WALKING PIECE OF ART

~

Poetry For Healing

DEANNA ARACELI

LA Casa de Luz

Copyright © **2024** by **LA Casa de Luz**

All rights reserved.

No portion of this book may be reproduced in any form without written permission from the publisher or author except as permitted by U.S. copyright law.

ISBN: **979-8-218-44170-8** (paper)

Cover by **Louise Androlia**

Illustrations by **Erin Masarajin**

To all the women who were silenced...

Contents

Part-I: Layers Unveiled
The Years Have Gone (13)
Lost Flower, Not Remembered (14)
Underneath the Veil (16)
Thoughts Go Astray (19)
Will You Stay? (20)
A Ray of Lost Hope (22)
Letter to You (24)
Deserving Better (26)
Underage (28)
The Door Unlocked (30)

Part-II: Sketches of the Self
Blank Sheet (36)
Another Day (38)
Loving False Perceptions (40)
Virtue (42)
Why Not? (44)
Time Flies (46)
See Within (48)
The Roller Coaster Called Life (50)
Forgive Myself (52)
Light Within Light Without (55)

Part-III: BrushStrokes of Becoming
Untitled (60)
Where I Belong (62)
Unity (64)
Awake (66)
Moments in the Past (68)
Fairy Tales (70)
In Disguise (72)
In the Rough (74)
Closer (76)
Him (78)

Divided into three parts:

Part I
Layers Unveiled

Part II
Sketches of Self

Part III
Brushstrokes Of Becoming

Introduction

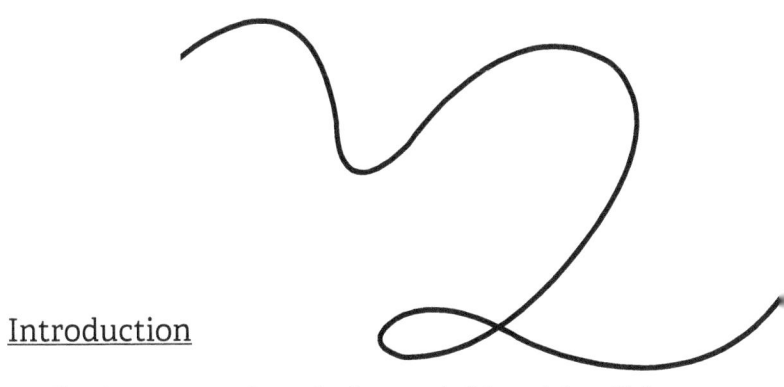

Healing is a process. It can be long, painful, and dreadful at times. It is much easier to cover the holes that have been shaped by traumatic experiences with comfort and suppression.

This booklet of poems is about doing the complete opposite—taking the hurt and transforming it into something creative. It is about stepping away from these experiences and observing them from afar, stopping being the victim, and accepting who we are before and after these things have happened to us.

I hope that as I come forward with these things, those who read can go within themselves and uncover those buried moments in their own lives.

Those moments where shame and guilt denied them of reflecting and learning from what had happened. So that we may not only accept and heal, but also move forward into sacred light. Then we will understand that these events do not make us who we are or shape the way we perceive the world, but call us to make it better.

I was one of them; I never spoke about such incidents until I was twenty years old.

I am fortunate to speak about such topics as I know there are many people who are forever silenced. This is for them, and this is for you. If any of this resonates within your core, know that someone is out there waiting for you to reach out and help their healing process begin.

So, let us begin…..

Part-1
Layers Unveiled

~

Trauma stored within the
subconsciousmind is illumined.

Deep-seated emotional wounds that remain hidden in the shadows. When we bring conscious awareness into our lives, we allow for the potential of healing and understanding of past experiences. There is transformative power in addressing and overcoming the layers of the story.

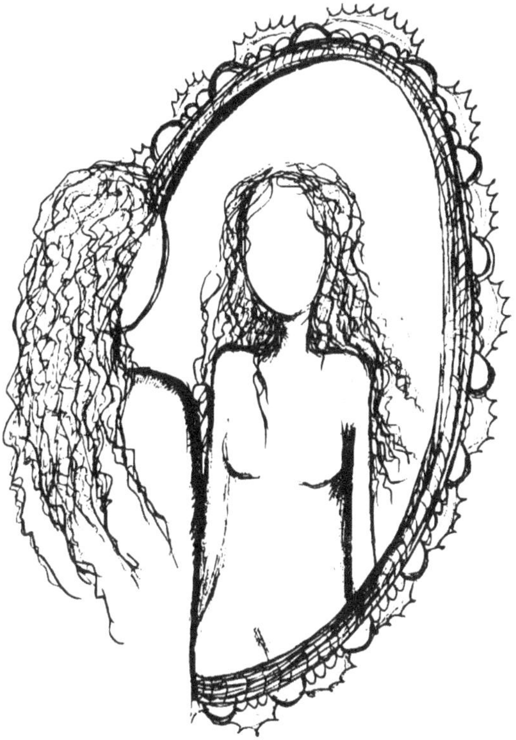

THE YEARS HAVE GONE

"Where have they gone to?" she questions.
"Oh, they passed away along with the seasons."
"Will they ever come back?" she persists.
"No, these things do not come back."
"Why not?" she continues.

"See, life is a journey.
You cannot hold that which has passed.
You can only learn from it and move forward."

"So I must walk away and never turn back?"
"Only turn to look if necessary, to remember, to feel."
"I want to, I want to move forward.
How shall I do so?"

"Write, flow with words, create art, express yourself.
Do not hide from the pain; feel it."
"I will," she reassures herself.

LOST FLOWER, NOT REMEMBERED

Cyclical circles spiraling all around.
Not lost and not found.
Remembrance is void as it was taken away from me.
One second of knowledge rather than pity.

Where has my mind gone?
To realms unknown in the mirror.
To thoughts of some distant past.
Torn away from all I knew,
I was left confused.
Scrubbing away the filth and dirt, inside, there was only hurt.

Violation against the body.
Falling into the hands of passion.
Calling me, pressuring me into tension.
Can I forgive myself?

Not the one on the outside, but her on the inside?
Naively creating escapes from the real pain she feels.

The world is on wheels.
Coming back to the place where we started
having accumulated some type of empathy for ourselves.
Letting go of the moment, which was not mine to begin with.

This is an illusion.
It's all a dream,
a wondrous myth.

UNDERNEATH THE VEIL

Time stopped when we glanced each other's way.
Butterflies swirling within,
that nervous feeling when you know it is all about to begin.

Who would have known he was a monster in disguise?
Looking for prey to speak his lies.
He hid them well, I must say.

So, who did I fall in love with?
He had no name.
He was behind a veil covering the truth.

I sunk back within myself, not knowing what to do.
Another case of the hopeless blues.
A world I tried to enter,
not knowing what lay in the center.

Flags sprung up, but I was too young to notice.
Happy someone loved me and was not afraid to show it.

He took advantage of my adolescence,
a boyish man I could not resist.
Sensuality was the interior of our dealings.
I was able and willing
to indulge in a sphere of oblivion.
With no concept of the world I was living in.

Blinded by lust,
with no reason, I just trusted
that this was real affection.

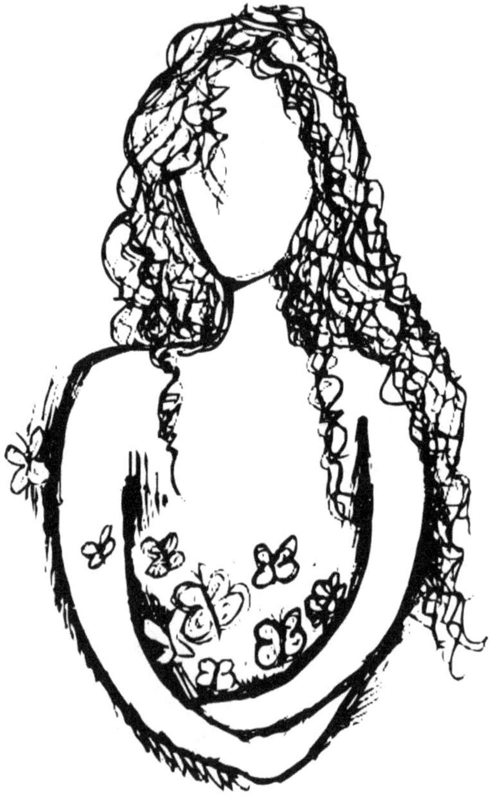

THOUGHTS GO ASTRAY

Why must I think life should be some way?
What gives me the right to have a say?

Tumbling down the spiral staircase of nescience.
Mistake after mistake, I have to get away.
Unnatural force upon my soul.
Give me all the things I lost at home.

The undesirable events that have taken place
within a span of years,
I have trouble understanding what I have left to give.

Of obstacles, traps, and cages, I must be aware.
Not to fall, but to hurdle over this despair.
Troubled and afflicted,
healing wounds that have been open for some time.

What do I have left to give if I'm not allowed to shine?

WILL YOU STAY?

Objects that make no sense.
Feelings of distress.
Taking away of innocence.

As you smile and lay.
No thoughts, no feelings, your way.
Touching the core of our beings.
You have no respect or dignity.

Toys you think we are.
To play and then toss away.

Useless.
Mindless.
Out of my control.
I thought once I had you, time would be no more.

As you walked away and never turned back.
I thought to myself, what is it that I lack?
Questions rushed into my naive mind.
Unwanted energy stuck within my spine.

You never truly loved me and I, not at all.
Friends spoke of the other side,
persuading me to join the ride.

No one spoke to me about these things.
Little did I know I was giving everything.

So as you continue, I try as well.
Knowing if you stayed,
I wouldn't have learned it this way.

A RAY OF LOST HOPE

Dragging luggage without weight.
Hypnotizing, but having nothing to say.
Creating an illusion of what could be.
Attaching emptiness for something fleeting.

Pleasuring outwardly and hurting inwardly.
Grabbing pieces to block what is supposed to be.
Shading the outline for false perception.
Heading in the wrong direction.

Leaving trails of sorrow
Not knowing if there will be a tomorrow.
Cutting away any love I have left.
Sitting on it and not letting me take a breath.

Allowing you to take me over for a second.
Noticing that you are just a pretender.
Filling in a hole that was never meant for you.

Trying to pick up the pieces of a ruptured heart.
You were just the spark among the flames.
You did nothing; I felt no shame.

Although I realized what I was missing all along,
It had nothing to do with you.
Nothing to do with me
but it was spirit and the in-between.

LETTER TO YOU

I'm sorry we met.
It was only two months, but I regret
leading you to believe that I could be her,
the one you introduce to your family.
Please understand me,
I was dealing with pain from another.

All I was looking for was a lover
and hope that he does not uncover
the lashes and thrashes that masked my heart.

Where could I have started
to confess the blood straining from my valves?
So I ran away
and locked the door with no word to say.

Wherever you're at, I hope luck has met you halfway.

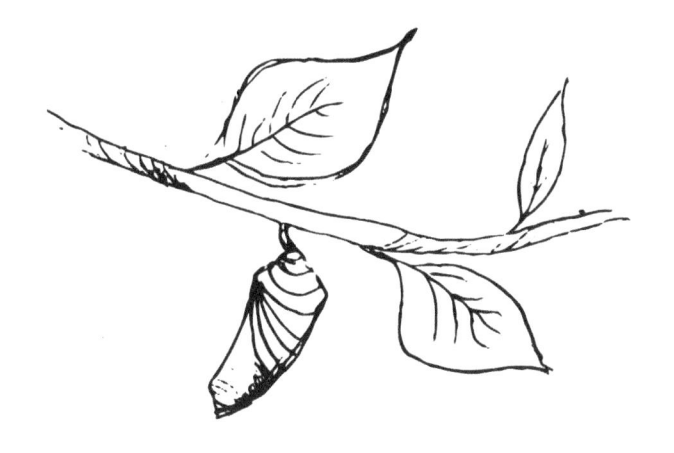

DESERVING BETTER

How many times have I settled for less?
How many times have I undressed my soul
for someone to stare back unimpressed?

How many times have I compared myself to keep his attention?
Because he stared too much in another's direction.

How many times have I cried myself to sleep?
And not one tear I wept,
did he ever say he would keep.

How many times did I wonder what to do?
To stay cool and not let him know I was a fool.
A fool for him or a fool for love,
any of the above.

How many times have I not seen my beauty?
Covered by society's standards
I keep undoing
the uniqueness of my creator.

I have slumped my shoulders,
thinned out my body,
and wore out my mind.

I slept it all away,
unaware of the time.

But one day, I took a look in the mirror,
the sun illumined and I could see much clearer,
that my happiness isn't defined by someone else,
my happiness isn't the making of external situations.

Happiness is found within,
in the silence of it all.
In the imperfection of my perfection.

I now understand why I settled for less so many times;
I didn't realize that I deserved the best.

UNDERAGE

She gives in to the pleasure down under.
She gives herself to one who is no better than the others.
Becoming one is now a fleeting joy.
She's just a girl.
He's just a boy.
Unknowingly meeting and keeping his aura for seven years,
Those memories will be hard to disappear.
Attachment will arise after the experience.

She doesn't know that each time
she gives a piece of herself away,
she is that much emptier,
And in turn, much more bitter.
"Don't give in unless you know the person
Beneath the facade,"
she reminds herself.

Walls have been built as her heart grows hard,
from the lovers she once knew.
Maybe she hardly remembers their face,
their name, the way their lips taste.
The way their body entered hers.

So far disconnected.
Now, love is just a play of fiction.
She cannot read between the lines.
She's just filling in the time
with Mr. Wrong.

Not listening to the voice droopy, weary, and long,
within her heart.
She's torn apart
from all that she knew.

Now, she draws caterpillars in their cocoons.
Hoping one day, she too, will have the courage to break away.
Become that butterfly and refuse to stay,
encapsulated in her pain.
She stands with dignity and walks away.

THE DOOR UNLOCKED

I have changed many wondrous times before.
Innocence ripped away from the childhood door.
No control or power to stop.

Just a little girl trying to sleep.
While he thought I was a piece of meat.
Fulfilling his perverted desire,
crying and trying to pull myself together.
Feeling weak and vulnerable, having no say.

Secrets hidden, and hate grew.
Disgust filled my body, and pain subdued.
You have no right to go about your life.
Death will meet you, it is true.

No longer will I stand silently waiting for heroes that do not exist.
I will fight my battles, win, and persist.

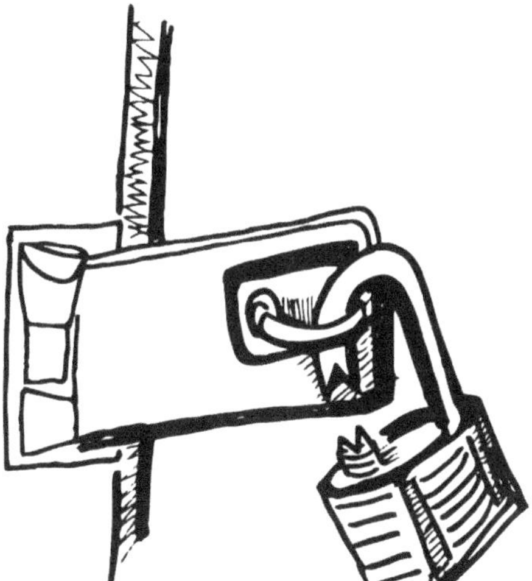

Part-II
Sketches of the Self

~

Healing the wounds left open.

Depth in layers in the process of healing the wounds left open. The contrast that it requires to uproot causes, process emotions, and rebuild a sense of security within. Self-reflection taken deeper into the process of patience and compassion. Playing a crucial role in the artist's embrace of self.

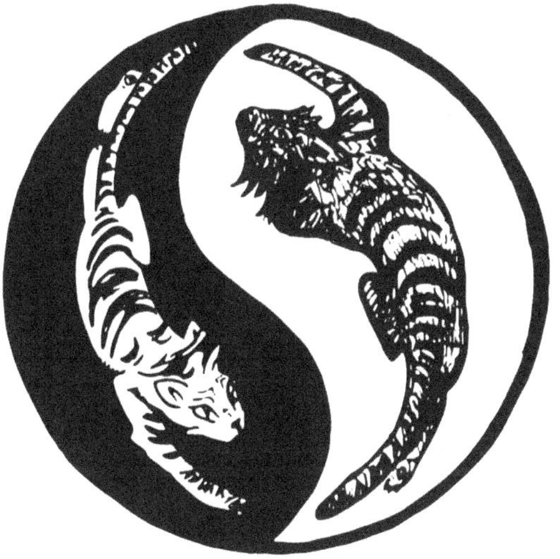

BLANK SHEET

Who was I before you?
Did I even have a clue?
I was so deep within me,
when I came to the surface, everything was empty.
Life, as I knew it, was a blank sheet.

Where shall I go?
Who shall I be?
Take the first step into an unknown reality.
Along the trail, I'll go,
beneath the bridge of show.

Pretentious, selfish, ungrateful,
things to let go.
I watch myself drifting
into the sea, I flow.

Unabiding, holding my breath.
Suffocating when I want to control
the things around me.
But I pause; I listen to the silence.

I remember the quintessence
of my being.
I take heed of my inhale
I deeply exhale and wait
to see that which lies underneath
of all I pretend to be.

Fake and unwilling to change,
it's easy to stay the same.
Unbreakable habits of conditioning.
Wallowing in my pain.

Pain that is not foreign.
Pain that is deeply rooted.
Why do I hide?
When if I step out of my pride
I'll see that I was always meant to illuminate the other side.

ANOTHER DAY

I walk with my head down; how can I feel pride?
I've made others feel the way I feel inside,
put people in the position of victim.
Every hurt, can they forgive them?
At what point do we regret it?
Or do we skip over that part?

Learning from each lesson and moving forward.
Doesn't matter how much you move,
take each step with hope.

What's on the other side of fear?
Why am I afraid to cope?
To accept myself for all my faults.
All the situations that have made me who I am today.

So, therefore, I do not have to lay
down on the ground with self-pity.
But I stand straight with my back against the wall.
A little timid because, at any moment,
I can fall into a hole.

A long way I'll go.
Into the world unknown.
Future experience awaits.
Take them by storm.
Never settle or become lukewarm.

LOVING FALSE PERCEPTIONS

Controlling sexuality.
What is left of me?

Thinking of my past,
my future,
my present.

Hurting inwardly, abusing outwardly.
What once was sacred has been taken,
thrown and tossed away.

Coming back to true romanticism,
the love that is not meant for this material world,
the love that is meant for the supreme being.

What stops me from this love?
Keeping attachment to that which is mundane.
Years have passed in vain.
Or have they?

Each day, I walk closer,
each day, things become brighter.
Walking towards the brilliance of illumination.
Seeking to rip away this lamentation.

Trust the ways of the saintly person,
who understands the essence of reality.

What we see,
don't believe,
it is all temporary.

Experience the limitations,
without attachment or expectation.
Find the lover of the soul,
who completes us and makes us whole.

VIRTUE

What does it mean to be virtuous?
Walking around this world, trying to be courageous.
Protecting myself in the concrete jungle.
Seeking shelter for this injured animal.

Sheep in wolf's clothing.
Can you see her?
Vulnerable inwardly, boldly standing,
having something to prove to the masculine.
Like the lioness prowling within.

When all I want to do is dive into the feminine.
Nothing is wrong with either as I traverse
this earthly plane one step at a time.
Finding true equality to hold both inside and still feel alive.

Yin and yang.
Positive and negative.
Balance, harmony, spirituality.

I'm not trying to rush since, chances are,
it will take some time.
But I keep hope as I cross that finish line.

WHY NOT?

Should I continue to think of the past with regret?
I should have done this,
I shouldn't have done that.

What's life if we can't make mistakes?
Are we allowed to plead for forgiveness?
Or will we always be shunned by those we hurt?
Did you not know?
When you hurt others, you hurt yourself in return.

Why must I go on this merry-go-round?
I'm sorry, but people won't forgive.
It's okay; spirit tells me to move on.
To find the new and drop the guilt.

Life at every moment offers a glimpse of adventure.
Why not take the risk?
Why not jump for joy?
Why continue living in sorrow, pain, and loneliness?

When you don't even know what will come next.
Trust your instinct.
Trust the voice within.

Don't allow the mind to be foggy with thoughts of shame.
Move past the ache,
move past the damage,
healing comes with time,
but we must be willing to do the work.

Go within and see the scars for what they are,
and rehabilitate with practice and patience.

Life does not pause when things don't go as planned.
Take it by the hand,
calm it with your tenderness,
never become inflexible.
Oh! There is so much more...

TIME FLIES

I'm learning a lot as time goes by.
No reason to hide behind the curtain.
All is not perfect or certain.
Life remains a mystery for those seeking meaning.
Getting caught up as if it's not real and you're just dreaming.

Multiple realities, this is the one I'm living.
I haven't even started yet; it's just the beginning.
Mistakes have guilted me in the past.
Words have shed layers of my being.
Healing and weeping,
there is no contrast,
just a heavy burden that won't last.

I've been here before,
I've felt this pain,
this ache that wakes me in the night,
the nightmares that have occurred more than twice.

Please lean in and listen,
I'm not looking for attention.
There are deep roots that have been left in the cold.
By now, they have grown dry and old.

Who is there to plant them once again?
I glance, and I see my reflection.
The perfection of misdirection.
She soothes and calms my soul.
She knows when I feel dreary and alone.
She reminds me to go back home.

To go to my nest where I am free.
To go to my nest where no one bothers me.
Trying to feel the wind and understand the ideas that float around my head.
Awakening before it is too late and I am dead.

Expansion of the inner world.
Shutting doors in the outer.
Vibrations of light fill the air.
Tell me, it is going to get better.

SEE WITHIN

Staring at the tip toes of my being.
What is happening?
Spinning in circles, I'm getting dizzy.
Don't worry, it's my history.

Where do I go now?
To a place called home?
Or am I just prone
to make mistakes and never understand why
everything seems so far away;
I don't know what else to say
I'm feeling like another person,
who was I the other day?

The other moment, the other minute,
all is past
be in the present
need not worry about the future.

The story only gets brighter.
Bright like the stars in the sky.
Bright like the moon shimmering from high.

Breeze touches my face,
my eyes glimmer with the radiance of green,
trees breathe, and land sleeps.

We are not here to crawl,
we are not here to bend.
We are here to extend
where we have been.

Let's come back
full circle, flow inward, and see within.

THE ROLLER COASTER CALLED LIFE

Keep your arms and legs inside, please.
Make sure your belt is safely secured.
Hold on to dear life; it's about to begin.
What you've been waiting for,

the   journey
within
        twists
              and   turns,
                                loops
and
surprises
        drops
                from
                high levels
                                    backward
                          diving.

Another turn into the unknown.
You fall, you scream, you want it to stop,
but then peace comes.
Gratitude, love, romance, adventure, discovery,
you're not wondering what will be next.

Moment by moment, you are savoring.
Devouring the pleasures surrounding.

Oh! Look there! The garden that's blooming.
Don't forget to smell the tulips as jasmines fill the air.

But once again, you turn into a dark corner.
Cobwebs meet you, memories buried, skeletons piled up.
"Don't be afraid," spirit answers your unasked question.

Each experience offers growth,
but when we don't breathe with hope,
fear is how we cope.

Transform the negative into the positive.
Be aware of the balance that lies between.
Not heard or seen,
but felt in the heart of the knower.
The true lover.
The one that can see above the lower.

FORGIVE MYSELF

I. Where can I begin?
As I sit within
these cage-like bars
that mirror and surround me.
Different bodies, different identities.
Which is me?
Which door have I opened?
Shall we see?

II. A slight knock, no one answers.
Cobwebs hide the knob,
brush away the dust, get ready to sob.
I know exactly where I am,
where I rarely visit.
It's dark and lonely there,
I'd rather not.
Files everywhere of different experiences.
I noticed this says 1960, but this body was born in 1990.

III. Truth is, I don't want to be here.
I don't want to relive this pain.

So, I'll say it,
there is no delay.
I have to forgive myself.

Go through all the shelves
and repeat,
"Even though these things have happened,
I choose to love and forgive myself completely."

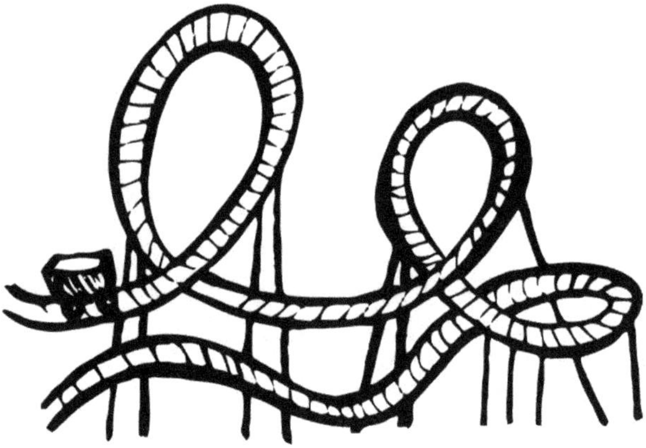

LIGHT WITHIN LIGHT WITHOUT

I want to be natural.
Natural in all that I do.
I need to be free.
Free in true love and devotion.
I seek harmony, balance, and peace.

I know not what comes next.
All I know is the past and now.
Things change when you least expect it.

Why should I hold back from a new experience?
Why should I hold back from a new beginning?
Life is a continuous process to the beloved.
There are no shortcuts, only detours and winding roads.

Take a step into the unknown.
Take my light into the darkness.
Take me away from myself.
Why must I continue to go on?
Because light is within and without.

Part-III
Brushstrokes of Becoming

~

Inspired by the world, inspiring the world.

Taking back our power to create positive change in our world. The ripple effect of the diversity of ideas, perspectives, and intentions. Fostering in magic to spark up. The energy to shine bright and find the balance between the dark and light. To find one's center, values, and integrity through the finishing touches of the art piece.

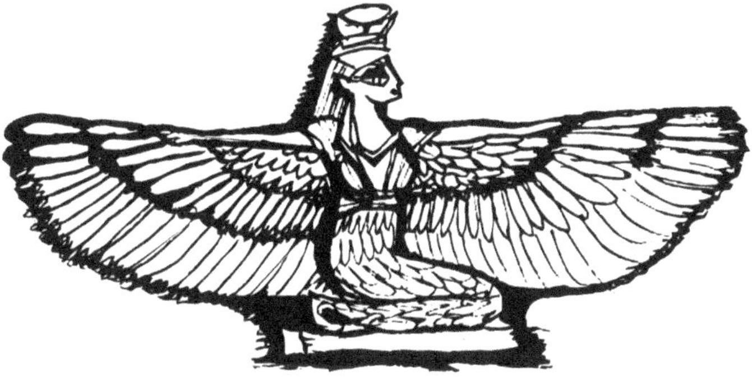

UNTITLED

Mysterious women
have something stirring within them.
They try to hide so no one can see them.
They shine so brightly
and are quite unaware
of the light they can share.

They step out of the corner,
come out of the dark,
and see that they illuminate everything.
No need to rush the creative force.

Nurture it to realize it is within reach.
See to it that you express,
not to impress,
but to undress the covering of the soul.
Reach down into places unknown.
Go where home is underneath the show.

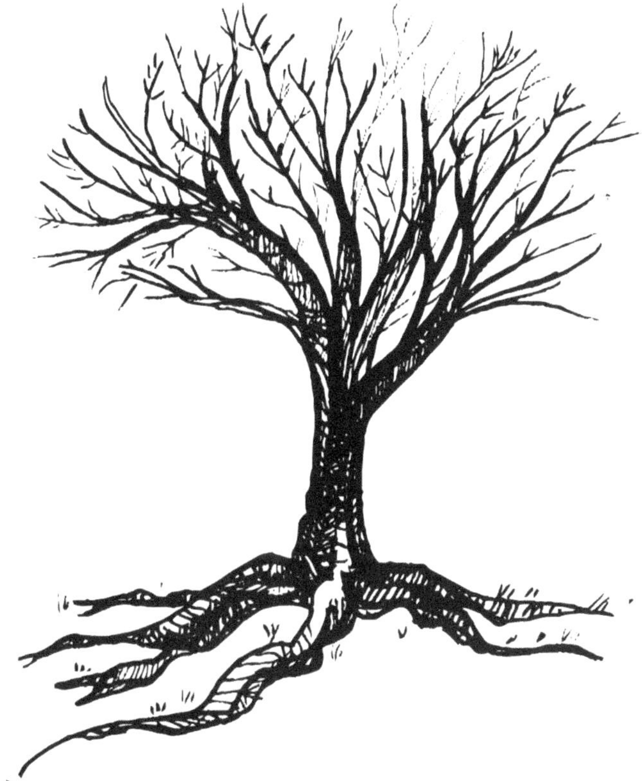

WHERE I BELONG

I belong to the wilderness,
where the weeds curve in whatever direction they feel,
where the sun shines a little brighter,
and the clouds dance in wonder.

I belong to nature,
where my feet are grounded,
where my spirit is connected,
and the wind gently holds me.

I belong to the earth,
where my body is calm,
where my being is strengthened,
and my fears dispelled.

I belong to myself,
where uniqueness is not a flaw,
where love always resides
and I don't have to try.

I belong to spirit,
where I see my true identity,
where I am immersed in peace,
and where everything comes at ease.

UNITY

The essence of learning
is to absorb knowledge
and live accordingly.

True knowledge brings one
in connection to their real self,
beyond the layers of bricks
built to let in no one else.

We are afraid of exposure,
to bring the darkness to light.
Ignorance keeps us bound.
We must stand up and fight!

What price can we put on education?
Isn't it our God-given right?

Nourishment to our intelligence,
feed the soul,
material coverings come and go.

But what remains?
Spirit inflamed.

Burning away selfish motives,
coming into contact with peaceful nature.
All creatures living in harmony,
voices coming together as a symphony.

As the light workers show us all we can be,
in connection with our divinity.
Arising as one while the sun rises
into the future of a new horizon.

This is the time to speak and live the Truth
discard the rest,
believe in all the things that together we can do!

AWAKE

Anxiety, why?
Unknown, unpleasant.
Future unpredictable.
Moments, only time is now.
Why ponder of the past,
when it's gone?
Let's change our perspective,
change our direction.

Listen to our intuition.
What language does it speak?
Language of feelings, emotions,
but deeper than the ones built by the mind,
but they are felt by the spirit.

Destroy barriers, boundaries,
limitations, and the cages built by our own hands.
Thoughts conceived by society and believed by the majority.
When will the blindfold fall?
Reveal the exact scene in which we live.

Beauty surrounds us, but buildings hide us.
4x4 rooms, no light, lost in grey.
Wake up to the color beyond the coffee stain.

Lost behind the screen
time elapses,
we've lost our youth,
now we stare at a body full of dust and pulled down by gravity.

Wasting time trying to show who we are
instead of being who we are.
Posing for our image of what happiness looks like.
Living in a facade with millions of followers.

Does that help us sleep at night?
Or does it keep us up as we conjure
what else we should do and say?

It's heavyweight; we must let go of the chains in our way.
Chase down our dreams and become awake.
Know the true meaning of life and live.
Don't be afraid; courageously jump into the darkness.
Your inner light will be your torch.

MOMENTS IN THE PAST

Inability to communicate,
it's easier to walk away.
Love cannot be forced.
You cannot force anyone to stay.
You cannot force anyone to speak.

It must come naturally from the core of the heart.
Where the soul lies,
where the knots and strings tie.
Attachment to an ideal rather than reality.
But can you see the difference between you and me?

You're afraid of places unknown.
I jump at the sight of risk and grow.
You're afraid to die alone.
I'm ready to dive into the memories so low.
You're afraid to give love a chance.
I'm awaiting the romance.

Now you see,

what can life be?

If we do not surrender on our knees.

Pray to the stars above to give us our needs.

Love is the epitome.

The greatest gift of all time.

The only way we will ever shine.

FAIRY TALES

Conditioned since the beginning.
Awaiting my prince in shining armor.
He will save me in my distress and dishonor.

Where is Phillip?
Aurora isn't herself without him.
Sleeping silently, hoping one day that kiss will set me free.
But what is true reality?

Love is a give and take.
You give, I take.
You take, I give.
Make the slightest mistake,
and we're off to the next.

You must meet me halfway,
or else I won't stay.
Half of the time, it's all just a game.
A game only the foolish play, they say.

If we expect to be completely satisfied by one person,
we are wrong.
No one can satisfy our spirit
besides the Great Spirit beyond.

Everyone else can meet our conditioned needs
but no further.
We have to look under
the veil that keeps us blind
to the fact that time
is just a factor that can't rewind.

So let us wake up to our true nature,
not expecting anyone to come and sweep us off our feet,
because those that we meet
are just helping our journey to become complete.

IN DISGUISE

Words can't speak
What lies beneath
The stars in the sky
It's all a bunch of lies
Truth comes in disguise
Waiting for us to open our eyes.

Peace I find when I look inside
The world is a mess, I'm trying to hide
From the dark corners
That leak under
The surface of attachment.

I hope that you haven't
Given up that which you seek
The door is open, just take a peek.

You have arrived
Just take a stride
Walk inside
Look around

The light is not bound
By earthly dimensions.

There is only one consideration,
Are you ready?
Have you become steady?
Take a leap
It's not so steep.

Don't be afraid,
the rest will be laid
down on the foundation of MAAT.
We are creating the plot.
Just withstand the laughs and the pain.

There is no gain,
if there is no transformation.
Cultivation of the correct stimulation.
Higher consciousness, the true self
is the secret of real richness and wealth.

IN THE ROUGH

Everywhere there is possibility,
one door closes, and the other unlocks,
slightly opens, so you may walk in.
So much light, you have to watch your step.
Blinded by the unknown, take a deep breath.

The guides come and go and change their disguise,
waiting to teach lessons, prepare you for the next situation.
People take off their masks so you can see their true colors,
with no limit of time,
Caring for people who never truly shared your interests.

It's okay because those change,
but you, you remain the same.
Those who see your beauty
will take every opportunity to love you,
unlike those only there when they get something in return.

Go back into yourself,
awake from the illusion, the dream of a wondrous world.
There are no mistakes; life moves forward.

Reality is no rainbow, but also not only a place for snakes.
Seeing past the hurt,
seeing the purpose behind the uncertainty.
Nowhere to go besides up,
when your perspective is grounded in the Earth.

No longer waiting for something to stir
within your heart,
everything falls into place or apart.
It's all a magical play,
don't know if you just began the first act or the last,
but go on as if it were a comedy, not a tragedy,
Change your direction and vision to fit
a life beyond the horizon.
Rise up and become a diamond.

CLOSER

The area closest to me is within.
Within a mind that has tried to intertwine
the sacred geometry of time.

Look through a window,
puppeteering, playing a role,
but what's beneath?

The soul.
No labels besides pure bliss, knowledge, and eternality...
Awaiting that person who has sustained
control over their senses.

Not allowing for their emotions to take over and blind them,
see through the confusion of pleasure and illusion.
Entangling in the webs of the old witch and noticing the glitch.

Find the missing piece,
turn on the switch.

Awaken to the Truth
you hold it all inside,
with the grasp of youth,
don't die before becoming alive!

HIM

Awakening to the person I have always been,
billions of eons have crossed to another second.

Time is relative,
to the situation we are in.

Ants live so long.
Humans are the same,
just trying to let go
of all the hidden pain.

How to express,
the words that have never been said?
Unraveled in my head.

But he looked right through me.
Not noticing the debris from thousands
of tragic moments of this life.

Cared for me,
loved me.
Taught me how to grow
and how to know.

My only shining light
in this tunnel that I thought would devour me.

My last breath makes it count,
chant the Holy names,
that's the only thing that can help!

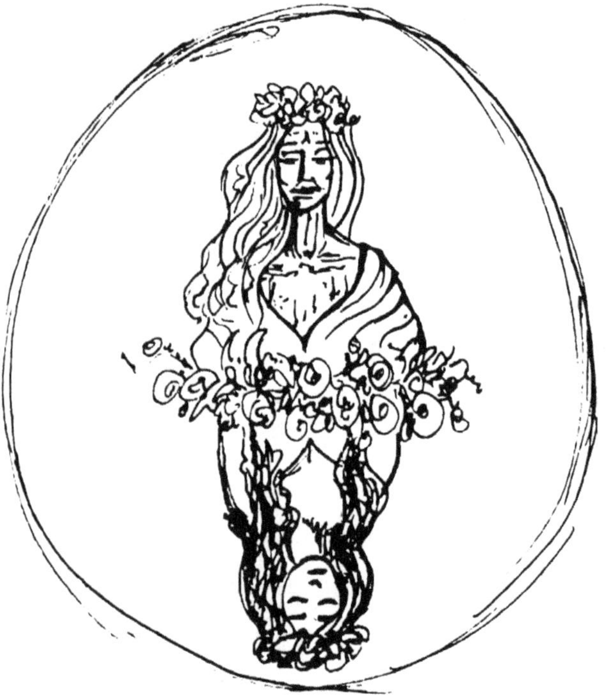

The End of the Beginning